HOPE
in Ageing

POETRY COLLECTION

FOREWORD BY
PAM RHODES

EMBRACING AGE
Later life in all its fullness

First published in 2023 by
Independent Publishing Network
Compilation © 2023 Embracing Age
Poems © individual poets
All rights reserved.

ISBN-13: 978-1-80517-052-5

info@embracingage.org.uk

embracingage.org.uk

CONTENTS

FOREWORD BY PAM RHODES 7

HOPE IN AGEING: AN INTRODUCTION 9

RASPBERRIES IN OCTOBER Jeremy Winter 14

WHERE'VE I LEFT THE CAR? Revd Kim Topham 18

WHAT DO YOU MEAN, HOPE IN AGEING! Elizabeth Ali 22

THE CHURCHYARD BENCH Michael Jackson 26

HOPE Matt MacKinnon Pattison 29

SEE THESE HANDS Julie Jordan 32

A BEACON OF HOPE Roy Boyson 34

ABUNDANCE Gill Bradbury 35

ACORN AND OAK Anne Woodcock 37

A LIFE FULL OF HOPE Dorothy McGuigan 40

BETTER THAN YESTERDAY John Buxton 41

BLACK GIRL ON THE BUS Michael Grannell 43

CELEBRATE Angie Pollard 45

ELMSIDE 2021 Mary Sanchez 47

FISH AND CHIPS FOR TEA Denise D'Souza 48

FRAMED BY A ZIMMER Jeremy Winter 49

FREEDOM Bob Kimmerling 51

HERE'S TO OLD AGE & A NEW BEGINNING Angela Davey ...52

HOPE IN AGEING Poetry Group at Priceholme Care Home 53

HOPE IN AGEING Lois Wiltshire 55

HOPE IN AGEING ACROSTIC Christine Truscott 56

HOPE IN AGEING. BREAD. Hermione Roff 57

HOPE IN AGEING RAP Jane Mennie 59

HOPE IN AGEING: THE WAY TO HOPE Jacqueline Hamblin ..61

HOPE WITHIN Brendan Conboy 62

HOPES AND DREAMS Jenny Betteridge 63

HOROLOGY Rose Marmion 65

I MAY BE OLDER Jackie Curtis 67

I MIGHT BE OLD Rosalie Grottick 69

I'M STILL ME! Susan Whiteford 71

IN HOPE WE TRUST Elizabeth Harrison 73

KEEP SMILING Connie Apps 75

LESS CONSEQUENCE Maria Therese Williams 76

LIFE'S SPAN Sue Whalley 77

LUXURIOUS LEISURE Jane Brocklehurst 79

MATRYOSKA Eirene Fargher-Smith 80

MY HOPE Neil Cooper 81

MY NEW ME Angie Pollard 82

NEVER STOP LEARNING Alexandra Wilde 83

OLD AGE ISN'T SO BAD Patricia Hammersley 84

OLDER? HOW DARE YOU! Elizabeth A Ali 85

ONCE A CREATIVE Christine Ratcliff 87

RECIPE FOR A HAPPIER OLD AGE Angie Pollard 88

SELF-SUFFICIENCY Ali Mitchell 90

SOUL REFLECTIONS Jeremy Winter 92

THANK YOU DEAREST EMILY Helen Mason 93

THE JOURNEY Olive Griffin 95

THE JOYS OF GETTING OLD Jean Carter 96

THE POINT OF AGE Paul Blackett 97

THE TOUCH OF A HAND Julie Jordan 99

THERE IS ALWAYS NEW HOPE Holly Trundle 101

TREES Ann Sangwin 102

UNOPENED GIFT Ian Curtress 103

USE IT OR LOSE IT, YOU CHOOSE IT Glenys Adams 105

WHEN I AM OLD AND SPENT Elisabeth Rosemary Coghlan 106

WHEN I WAS BORN Henk Van Oort 108

WHEN WE LEAST EXPECT IT John Buxton 110

YOUR WAY William Barnett 112

FOREWORD BY PAM RHODES

When EMBRACING AGE first suggested the idea of a poetry competition on the theme of "Hope in Ageing" and asked me if I would join Dave Bilbrough and Amanda Root on the panel of judges, I was thrilled to accept. I must admit, though, as someone who is a comfortable seventy-something now, I did wonder whether most pensioners today would come up with many different adjectives to describe the experience of growing older, but the word "hope" might not feature amongst them.

How wrong I was! More than two hundred entries poured in to present us with a sublime tapestry of insights, feelings and experiences through which hope is solidly threaded, weaving together life, limb, laughter and love.

There's a lot of laughter. Our writers laugh at themselves, recognising that as time marches on, memory seems to march away with it. We forget things. We're befuddled by technology. Sometimes our joints ache and our limbs don't work as they used to. All too often, conversations are held around us, rather than with us, which can leave people in the autumn of their lives feeling irrelevant and even invisible.

But this collection is a glorious celebration of all that our later years can bring. Our writers have been wonderfully creative, skilful and imaginative as they each embrace age in their own way. They speak of the inspiration to be found in nature, the pleasure of good company, as well as the contentment to be discovered in simply being alone. Mind you, these poets don't hold back in telling it like it is - the inconvenience, the indignity and, all too often, the fear of growing older – but I'm left with an overwhelming feeling of hope as their words swell with thankfulness for the blessing of life itself.

And their sense of the faithful presence of God, who has walked with them through the years, who brings comfort to them now, and who one day will welcome them home, brings reassurance and hope to us all.

HOPE IN AGEING: AN INTRODUCTION
TINA ENGLISH, DIRECTOR OF EMBRACING AGE

Hope is probably not the first word that springs to mind when you think of ageing. Society bombards us with such negative views about the onset of grey hair and wrinkles, whilst promoting a smorgasbord of lotions and potions to keep up looking young.

At Embracing Age, we believe that you don't need to feel downhearted about the process of ageing, or try to fight it. Rather, you can embrace growing old, enjoying its fruit and savouring the joys of later life. But don't take our word for it. In 2023, we organised the Hope in Ageing poetry competition, inviting anyone over 50 years old to share their verse on this theme. We had over 200 entries and several common threads emerged.

New opportunities and more time, entwined with a more carefree attitude to life are mentioned as sources of hope: time for leisure activities, to learn new things, to reflect, to give back and to impart wisdom. Time spent with family and friends brought hope, with a fresh valuing of friendship, and, along with hope, joy was reaped from being with grandchildren and seeing future generations develop.

Others wrote of ageing bringing new perspectives and a desire to live life to the full, enabling them to appreciate the little things and see each new day as a blessing.

Faith emerged as an important source of hope in ageing, with more time to spend praying, or resting in God's presence, and a fresh awareness of Jesus being alongside on the ageing journey. Others wrote of the hope of Heaven, and life beyond the grave when ageing bodies and minds would be renewed.

The beauty and the healing power of nature were a further source of hope in later life, with more time to smell the flowers and delight in the wonder of creation.

I resonated with many of these themes, as I am sure you will too. As a follower of Jesus, I echo the hope that springs from faith. I love what the Bible says about hope (Hebrews 6:19) in this context, describing it as "an anchor for the soul, firm and secure."

You might be interested to know what the writer of Hebrews had in mind when he wrote about hope. The Hebrew word for hope literally means a cord or a rope. A few years ago, my husband preached a sermon on hope and brought along his climbing rope as a visual aid. My family are really into climbing - I'm not, but I have watched them on many occasions!

When you climb, you wear a harness with a rope attached to it. The other end of the rope goes through a special pulley device (a belay) that is attached to a second person who is on the ground. That person holds the rope securely, giving it some slack so that you can climb to greater heights, and then tightening it so that should you fall, you won't drop very far, or hit the ground. The climber has total confidence in the rope to support them if they lose their grip and in the person on the ground who is in control of the rope. There is an expectation and a confidence that they can climb and will be held if their foot slips. In the same way, I have found that there is a certainty to the hope that comes from following Jesus – it anchors my soul through the seasons and storms of life.

The Bible contains lots of promises about many things – some related to ageing and life beyond the grave. In the Psalms, older age is described as a time of fruitfulness: "They will still bear fruit in old age, they will stay fresh and green". Furthermore, should we reach a stage of frailty, God assures us, "Even to your old age and grey hair I am he. I am he who will sustain you. I have made you and I will carry you." And then, about life beyond the grave we are reminded of "an inheritance that can never perish, spoil or fade. This inheritance is kept in heaven for you". About heaven we are promised: "He will wipe every tear from their eyes. There will be no more death or mourning or crying or pain".

There is much to hope for, both in this life and the hereafter. As you read these poems may they bring a smile to your face, and ignite hope in your heart as you continue your journey of ageing.

We have placed the three winning poems first, followed by each judge's highly recommended poem, along with the judge's comments on these six poems and a little information about the poets. The remaining shortlisted poems are presented in alphabetical order.

THE POEMS

RASPBERRIES IN OCTOBER
JEREMY WINTER (64)

As summer turns to autumn
And the leaves begin to fall
Nature seems to tire
And the birds begin to call

Summer warmth recedes
The nights are getting colder
Winter won't be far behind
Squirrels become bolder

We gather in the harvest
Pick grapes from the vine
Hedgerows gleam with berries
And rosy apples shine

Summer fruit, which seems so good
Has gone, we think in haste
But raspberries in October
Still give surprising taste

Life also has its seasons
In youth we reach our prime
But later years bring something new
A more reflective time

Embracing Age

Our memories and experience
Have much to teach and show
As energy begins to ebb
Our pace begins to slow

Mistakes we've made have taught us well
Our gifts and talents found
Our strengths we've tried to put to use
Our weaknesses renowned

As time slips by we wonder
Are the skills we have still needed?
When all is new and older voices
Often go unheeded

But don't give up, at least not yet
We still have much to do
We can't be sure what's coming next
Adventures to pursue

As new life takes the place of old
Change will come and then
Those raspberries in October
Will make us think again

JUDGES' COMMENTS:

DAVE BILBROUGH WRITES:

This evocative poem grabbed my attention right from the start. The vivid description of summer, turning eventually to autumn, had me questioning, at first, its relevance to the theme. Then, beautifully, it opened out as a parallel of a life well lived through seasons and years. I loved it - it is a worthy winner.

AMANDA ROOT WRITES:

This is a beautiful poem. The poet leads us through the changes in the seasons as similar to the seasons of older age. Our later years bring something new, a more reflective time, a time when the pace of life slows and we wonder "are the skills we have still needed?" There is great wisdom and a surety running through the poem. The poet encourages us not to give up, and we are stirred into a real sense of hope. The return to the image of the raspberries in the final stanza, both breaks our heart and inspires us to go forward.

PAM RHODES WRITES:

I love this poem because comparing the span of our lives to the rhythm and wonder of the seasons is such a clever way to illustrate the strengths, beauty, battle and wisdom we share with all of God's creation. And I remember so well the treat of finding a ripe juicy raspberry in the garden, with its bright red promise of delicious flavour – and to recognise that same sense of delight now as we grow older is something to treasure as the years go by.

ABOUT THE POET

Jeremy is 64, originally from Shropshire, but has lived near Preston in Lancashire for most of his adult life. He has worked as a social worker and manager in the field of Adults with Learning Disabilities for over 30 years and is also a qualified Counsellor. He is married with three grown up children and one grandchild, with another expected soon! He enjoys cycling, hill-walking, photography and gardening. He has been writing poetry for just over 10 years, which he finds is a very helpful way to express his thoughts and feelings about significant life events. The title of the poem, Raspberries in October, came to him after being surprised to find some very late ripening raspberries in the garden. This made him reflect about how older people still have much to offer, which eventually led to this poem being written.

WHERE'VE I LEFT THE CAR?
REVD KIM TOPHAM (60)

Well, what a state to be in, I can't see very far
I've lost the will to learn much tech, and where've I left
the car?
I don't know how to Twitter and TikTok ain't much
use
My hearing aid fell out again and my teeth are working
loose.

Can't find a pen, who took my phone, I know I left it
here
When on a trip, my only thought's, I hope the toilet's
near!
Can't get the jam jar open, the top shelf's far too high
And when I find a parking space, I give a thankful
sigh.

But frankly speaking, it's not too bad, this thing of
growing old
There's lots of time for holidays, on beaches coloured
gold
Or lying in or meeting friends or wearing hats, so bold
Or having time to clean the tiles of all that nasty
mould.

With time to spend with children and children's
    children, more
The laughs we have by building tents and lava on the
    floor
We go on walks and meet for drinks and dance the
    whole night through
It's amazing just what one can do, with an orthopaedic
    shoe.

Time is what we're given, whether short or whether
    long
It's what we try to make of it, that makes it right or
    wrong
I know that when I'm finished, my Lord will take me
    far
My hope is in Christ Jesus, but where've I left the car?

JUDGES' COMMENTS:

PAM RHODES WRITES:
Was the Revd. Kim Topham watching when I did LOSE the car in Asda's car park just the other week? Every line of this poem echoes with me – the aches and pains, and not being able to get on with technology without an eight-year-old by my side! We all loved this poem with its delightful mix of humour and unfortunate fact – and especially for the writer's own joy in living that shines through every line.

DAVE BILBROUGH WRITES:
I loved the shape of this poem. Early on we get the question then it's repeated again at the end. Throughout there are details of everyday predicaments we can all identify with. This lighthearted but thoughtful romp made me laugh out loud and savour the humorous side-effects of growing older.

AMANDA ROOT WRITES:
A gloriously funny poem tackling the many challenges of ageing in a light-hearted way, but managing to keep the message profound. There is a real sense of energy and resilience that shines out from this poem.
Forgetfulness, physical limitations and age-related anxieties are paralleled with the consolations to be found in holidays, time with grandchildren and friends, dancing, and ultimately a future with Christ which

serves as an anchor to the whole piece. The final message is dealt in delightful juxtaposition to the lost car so we do not dwell, we feel cheered on and rallied by our mutual experience.

ABOUT THE POET

Kim has four children and lives in Clent. She is a parish priest of three churches, as well as the operations manager for the local community shop and cafe. So life is busy!

A friend sent her the link to the poetry competition and she thought she'd have a go.

WHAT DO YOU MEAN, HOPE IN AGEING!
ELIZABETH A ALI (68)

Why do you see only lines and wrinkles,
Grey thinning hair and sagging muscles?
Think not the outer reflects the inner,
Look into the eyes, watch out for the smile,
Listen for laughter and feel that warm touch
And know that this wizened and hobbling old crone
Can still beat you at chess, make new things from old,
Turn dust into verdure and house into home.

Take care how you denigrate stories we tell,
Look under the words and take note of the theme,
A timely parable may just save your skin,
Though not one of us knows if, or when, that might be.
Still, remember the rhythm of life carries on
As long as the heart beats, the tears flow,
The love swells, the Spirit within continues to grow,
No stifling demon can rule in my soul.

The blossoms of spring and the colours of fall,
The kind warmth of summer and fresh bite of frost
Continue to stir, in us all, a response,
Come what may, come what will,
The life force gives hope still
Whatever fate chooses to throw in our way,
We lived once, we yet live, responsible, bold,
Ideas still burgeon, no matter how old.

JUDGES' COMMENTS:

AMANDA ROOT WRITES:
This is a wonderfully passionate poem and offers a challenge to the reader to look beyond what we see, to listen, to consider the skills and abilities of older people, the inner rather than the outer. I loved the energy behind the rhythm, drawing us beyond the obvious signs of ageing, the easy judgements, to the affirmation that 'As long as the heart beats... love swells, the spirit continues to grow.' The sure declaration 'No stifling demon can rule in my soul' rallies and lifts us into the stirring positivity of the final lines; 'Come what may, come what will...' we have a response to the beauty around us, ideas still burgeon and the life force gives hope, no matter what our age.

DAVE BILBROUGH WRITES:
For me, a good poem needs to be felt as well as heard. Using a cascade of words and turns of phrase Elizabeth offers a fierce, bold defiance against the typecasting so many hold as they look at those in later life. The wisdom and resilience of our older generation were the key themes raised within me as I meditated on the expressive poem.

PAM RHODES WRITES:
For me, this poem was outstanding in the glorious hope that underpins every thought and line in these beautifully-written verses. We all know that, as we notch up the years, we find ourselves cherishing every

moment and experience – and the lines we see in our own face in the mirror are testament to all we've been through, learned, failed at and valued most dearly. We've loved life – and with the wisdom gleaned along the way, we love life even more when we finally have the time to enjoy it to the full in our later years.

ABOUT THE POET

Elizabeth was born in Yorkshire and always loved song, poetry and stories. At age nine she first read 'Jane Eyre' – she was living near Haworth at the time. At University in Guildford she ran a writing group called Quill (Quite Unusual Institute of Literary Loons).

She became a midwife and loved the privilege of helping lovely women to bring new life into the world. She ended up with two babies of her own and two in the next generation. She did continue 'scribbling', including an attempt at novel writing, which was far too demanding whilst doing a job full-time and running a home.

Since retiring, she meets regularly with a small group of writers and it was through this group that she learnt of the Embracing Age competition. The poem was, initially, a rant on the idea that there could be any need for 'hope' in her ageing process. Once she had read up on the charity, she readjusted and managed to suppress her critical attitude to the theme, but decided the title of her poem should still reflect a little of her initial reaction.

Who surround in constant witness,
Evince the timeless.

So, as you gently share your peace,
I shed fears of constraining years, trusting
Tears and pains be wiped with God's
Heavenly promise.

PAM RHODES WRITES:

Throughout my decades of presenting 'SONGS OF PRAISE', I've sat on so many benches in so many churchyards that this bench feels like a dear and familiar old friend. We've shared a catalogue of feelings as we've sat together, often battered by life, but with my face lifted towards the sun – just as Michael Jackson finally lifts our hearts and souls towards God's "heavenly promise". This beautiful, perceptive poem rang warm chords of memory and recognition in me.

ABOUT THE POET

Michael is a retired Anglican priest, now in his eighth decade. One of the great joys of later life for him is time spent with his seven grandchildren, although he sees less of the two who live in Australia. He was for twenty-six years director of a Christian charitable foundation providing sheltered housing and nursing care for older people. This has given him a great interest in how we can age well and draw on the spiritual resources which help us to a fulfilled old age.

He decided, in retirement, to write about his thoughts on this process and his book "Still Love Left: Faith and Hope in Later Life" was published a couple of years ago. He drew quite extensively on poetry in his book, and as an occasional poet himself welcomed the chance to enter the Embracing Age poetry competition. Walking his dogs takes him through the churchyard of his local parish church and he often spends a short while sitting on a particular bench there, and just appreciating the peace of the moment. When the poetry competition was announced, he was struck by the affinity between himself and that aged bench which offered him such regular support. From this initial thought his poem flowed very naturally. He hopes it strikes a chord in those who read it. The bench is as delighted as he is to be commended!

HOPE
MATT MACKINNON PATTISON (98)

When Hope fades,
  Then Faith - in angry doubt
  Turns hermit
  In the backwoods of suspicion,
  And Love - a prisoner caught
  In lonely tangled web
  Of self pity.
When Hope dies
  And Love
  No longer free to give,
When Hope dies
  Can Faith
  Itself have long to live?

When Hope survives,
  A single distant star
  In darkest night
  Blinking out its message,
  "The purpose cannot fail."
Then Faith renewed
  Awaits the morning light,
And Love - unfettered,
  Runs to meet the dawn
  Of promise.

AMANDA ROOT WRITES:

This poem really captivated me. It is beautifully considered, expertly crafted, and each image carries us into a depth beyond words. Simple statements pose two different relationships to Hope and how these influence Faith and Love. "When hope fades" sees Faith as a hermit dwelling in 'angry doubt', and Love as a prisoner caught in 'self pity'.

In sharp contrast, "When Hope Survives" offers an alternate view. The single distant star in the "darkest night" resonates in its profound simplicity. The solitary, fragile "blinking out" of the message "The purpose cannot fail" sparks a light of hope in the reader. Faith is then renewed, and Love, released from its bonds, runs to meet the dawn of promise.

ABOUT THE POET

Matt has learned a thing or two about hope during his long and varied life. Born in 1924, on a street called Rotten Row, he spent his early years in an orphanage, following the death of his mother during childbirth. He joined the army in 1942 and saw action in Algeria and Italy. He started in the infantry and was subsequently chosen for the SAS.

After the war he was sent to Germany, where he served with a war crimes investigation unit. He married in 1948 and worked as a labourer while he studied at night school to become a draftsman. He progressed to engineering and management, designing and constructing oil rigs, power stations and other heavy engineering.

He was also a Methodist minister and enjoyed writing poems as part of his sermons. He describes how he sits down and the words just come to him.

SEE THESE HANDS
JULIE JORDAN (64)

See these hands, they once held you,
Precious baby, soft and new.
All my hopes and dreams I'd share
Whilst you slept without a care.

See these hands, they cooked and sewed,
Cleaned and knitted, bore the load
Then clasped together, daily prayer,
Faith and trust, my God is there.

See this face, it tells a story,
Sometimes pain and sometimes glory.
Wisdom behind eyes of watery blue
Faith, hope and love has seen me through.

See this face, its smiles and frowns,
Reflecting all life's ups and downs.
A life well lived, a job well done
Now time for peace, the race is run.

See this hair, not fair but grey.
Crowning glory fades away.
But one day when I'm oh so old,
I'll trade this silver crown for gold.

DAVE BILBROUGH WRITES:

Hands are such personal things. Everybody's got them and everybody's are unique. As a seasoned guitar player day by day I look down on mine and over the years see subtle changes as they 'weather' through the passing of time. I really like the way Julie uses the opening phrase 'See these hands' as the touchstone for her poem here, sighting various life activities along with a growing sense of experience gained as she ages through the years with her descriptions of hands, face and hair leading up to the great hope that is to come.

ABOUT THE POET

The inspiration for Julie's poem was her beloved Gran, Mary.

She was so gentle and loving, and her hands were always busy caring for her family. Even latterly, when confined to a wheelchair, she still crocheted baby blankets right to the end.

Julie used to call her "My angel without wings", but at last she gained them when she went to Glory

A BEACON OF HOPE

ROY BOYSON (97)

I have seen wildflowers
Grow in hard rocky places
Smiles light up tired old faces
Wit and Wisdom found
From the elderly and unprofound
Admired their survival skills
Despite those prevailing ills -
Had kindness from strangers,
Beauty from what seemed ugly,
Joy from Spontaneity
The sudden shimmer and glimmer of sunlight
Ripples and reflections by rivers
Pleasure and Surprise
From Music's 'Anon' and 'Trad'
To gentle away the Sad -
So I Hope Still...

ABUNDANCE
GILL BRADBURY (75)

Abundant worry, abundant care,
depleted income, thinning hair,
abundant problems with IT,
depleted brain cells, you'll agree.
Abundant problems with my knees,
pass me my stick, I'm asking, please.
I know I put my keys just here
but in a trice they disappear.
The things I thought that I once knew,
I've bidden them a fond adieu.
Unlike the pounds around my waist
that are less easily erased.

Abundant time to spend with friends
a bunch of old comediennes.
Abundant talk of days gone by,
Times full of laughter, times we'd cry.
Grandkids who love to be with me,
an ever growing family tree.
All those books I never read
now find a place beside my bed.
There's time for new creative skills
or even daring theme park thrills.
Taking time to see the view,
new vistas or ones I once knew.
Listen to music, sing or play
those favourite songs from yesterday.

Hope in Ageing

Or p'raps I'll just make up my own;
it's true, with practice, skills have grown.

My garden brings such joy and treasures,
heavenly scents and visual pleasures.
Cuppa or glass in contemplation
while thinking of my next vacation;
not obliged to make it camping,
a cruise the thing on which I'm banking.
Someone else to cook and clean
leaves me free to primp and preen;
free to give my time away
to those who pass the time of day.
My blessings I am free to share
and offer up a little prayer
for worried souls and busy too
with far too much on hand to do
and know the privilege is mine;
abundance for all is God's design.

ACORN AND OAK
ANNE WOODCOCK (60)

Together, one bright autumn day, they set out to plant
An acorn they'd found in the litter of leaves on the
    green,
Where she'd scurried around like a busy human
    squirrel
While he sat on the bench under the regal oak
To catch his breath and view the familiar scene.

His tremulous hand struggled to steady the pot;
Her small chubby fist tightly gripped the battered
    spoon,
But she managed to tumble in most of the compost and
    then
Poked a hole with her finger and dropped in the nut,
    and they both
Patted it down nice and snug, and the job was done.

They only went to the green again one more time,
Now that cold, wet winter weather was setting in.
Side by side they sat in rare sunshine. He got her to
    think:
Where would the acorn now be that had birthed that
    huge tree?
Wide-eyed, she heard him say every trace would be
    gone.

At first, on each visit to see him, she'd study the pot.

Hope in Ageing

Her fingers would tingle—she so longed to dig it all
    up,
Avid to know what was going on underneath,
Since all she could see was the same old rain-soaked
    humus,
But he told her, for now, they must let the acorn sleep.

Then soon she forgot all about the acorn they'd
    planted.
The pot stood outside through sunshine and frost and
    squall.
It must have been May when she happened to be there
    one morning,
And the carer brought it inside so they both could see
A bright green shoot erupting out of the soil.

From then on she'd always insist that they both check
    the pot;
Together they saw the leaves sprout and grow over the
    rim.
But one day he'd gone… Someone said he had fallen
    asleep,
His body too tired to live in this world anymore.
Uncomprehending, she took the new seedling home.

Years later, she went to his grave to look at the
    headstone,
Recalling his voice and so many things she'd been told,
Imagining his worn-out old body laid under the earth,
Just like the acorn they'd long ago planted together,

Now knowing that's simply what happens when we
    get old...

Remembering his chuckle, the way his eyes twinkled,
    his bright-sunbeam smile
And their own secret code and his stories—the simple
    affection
That rooted and sheltered her. Where now had all of
    that gone?
If all of it were only acorn, then what might the oak be?
And she realised he'd cherished the best hope of all:
    resurrection.

A LIFE FULL OF HOPE

DOROTHY MCGUIGAN (91)

Age is just a number,
I am so often told
But with aches and pains and replaced joints
I know that I am growing old.

As each day dawns I am full of hope
That all is well with those I love.
That wars will end and peace descend
Minds will heal and hearts will mend.

Hope and prayers are all I can offer,
For a world that is battered by evil intent,
As each day dawns and new life begins
We have time to look back and repent our sins
Not to a life that is slowly ending
But to a future of life full of hope that is ascending.

BETTER THAN YESTERDAY
JOHN BUXTON (58)

Awake just before sunrise
recurring thought in my mind
a desire for a new experience
every day the same mundane existence
push the boundaries say I
a new adventure
seize this day
to make a difference in some way
help me make today
better than yesterday.

Share my love of walking
a freedom I hold dear
let us venture forth
seek out a mystery pathway
London so rich in areas of natural beauty
waiting to be discovered
along the river Thames and beyond
push the boundaries say I
captivating, glorious panoramic views
making us feel energised, alive.

I desire an open space
nature's healing energy
fly a kite, wave at a canal boat, bird watch
sit under a flourishing tree
freedom of spirit released

push the boundaries say I
shadow of dementia kept at bay
returning refreshed, invigorated
enlightened by a day
better than yesterday.

BLACK GIRL ON THE BUS
MICHAEL GRANNELL (77)

Black girl on the bus,
The 89,
Lewisham to Bexleyheath.
You look so smart
In your school uniform.
How old are you?
14 or 15?
You don't know it yet,
But you are the future.

Old white guy on the bus,
The 89,
Lewisham to Bexleyheath.
You look neat but tired
In your summer coat.
How old are you?
70 or 75?
You know that most of your future
Is past,
But there's still a bit left.

Facing one another at the back
Of the 89
From Lewisham to Bexleyheath.
So close that
Your knees might touch,
But of course, they don't.

Hope in Ageing

You sit aslant
With eyes averted.
You are both British.

You share this journey
On the 89
From Lewisham to Bexleyheath.
The girl thinks fondly of her Grandad
In Nigeria,
And the man of his Granddaughter
In Australia.
You share much more
Than you think.
The future is full of hope.

CELEBRATE
ANGIE POLLARD (68)

Celebrate your waking - another day alive!
Take joy in finding little things to help you grow and
    thrive.
So what if fingers fumble, or drop a cup or two?
They still know how to do their work: they still belong
    to you.

Eyesight isn't what it was, it's sometimes hard to see,
But that beauty in the mirror shouts, "Hello, girl, it's
    me!"
I can't now see the wrinkles in this lovely face of mine.
I celebrate my short sight - I've never looked so fine.

So I celebrate my body, it's all I've got, you see.
I'm grateful that I'm breathing and I'm happy to be me.
I now look back in wonder at my life, still rushing by.
Who knows what's in the future? But whatever is, is
    mine.

I'm excited for tomorrow, today has just been great.
I'm thankful for the yesterdays, I'm no longer going to
    wait.
No, my life is just beginning, a new adventure has
    begun.
Tomorrow holds excitement, I've decided I'll have fun.

The world is there for taking: I won't let doubts hold
    me back.
Grab every opportunity; may every hour be packed.
I'll find joy in every sunrise, I'll throw smiles at
    everyone.
I'll laugh at every mishap: against ageing, I'll have
    won.

ELMSIDE 2021
MARY SANCHEZ (87)

Menaced by deadly virus,
Cut off from kith and kin,
We seek the healing power of nature,

The garden beckons us.
Towering trees, shrubs and flowers
enfold us as we step into their embrace.

There we sit in a sunlit yard
and gaze at a blackbird pecking at crumbs
left from teatime cakes,
and silence is broken by the
joyful songs of our feathered friends.

We amble down a hidden path
and at its end are dazzled by
a mass of peonies with crimson velvet petals.

A lush, green lawn lies before us
bordered by myriad shrubs clothed
in delicate flowers.

And thus we sit and gaze in peace,
soothed by the healing power of nature.

FISH AND CHIPS FOR TEA
DENISE D'SOUZA (57)

Norman, patting his stomach, pipes up with glee,
'I hope that we have fish and chips for our tea.'
'Oh yes,' says Valerie, 'and ice cream for pud.
A little of what you fancy does you good.'

My mind flashes back in its odd little way.
I see you and me, Daisy, as clear as day,
Holding our noses in the school dinner queue.
I sniff with a shudder. 'I hope it's not stew!'

It's funny peculiar (as my Tom would say)
How memories return you thought faded away.
Though I may forget even you, Tom my dear,
We live in the hope of our love shining clear.

The most I hope for is my knees don't give way,
And something to do and enjoy in each day.
Says Annie, 'When I see the first spring flowers bloom,
I'm hopeful that summer will be along soon.'

I see hope in spring flowers too. But far more
I hope to have someone I love to care for.
I hope, more than there's fish and chips for my tea,
To always have someone who cares about me.

FRAMED BY A ZIMMER
JEREMY WINTER (64)

Away on holiday, trying to relax
Seeing the word 'zimmer' takes me back
Home to where a zimmer frame stands
Too big for my Mum, too high for her hands

Seeing her struggle and clearly in pain
Trying to be positive, looking for gain
Long-standing faith giving way now to fear
Beckoning future might soon be here

Caring for others, still full of love
Now it's time to receive care from above
Delivered through others, family and friends
With advice from professionals on whom we depend

Confidence draining and energy less
Hard to find a way through the mess
But coming together, out of the muddle
A picture emerges, like a jigsaw puzzle

Faith rises daily and hope is returning
Energy growing and new lessons learning
Can't see the end, but trying to trust
Each step's a new one, trying's a must

Give it a go, lean on your zimmer
Lean on God more, let's see a glimmer

Hope in Ageing

Of all that's in store around the next turn
New things to experience, new wonders discern

Don't take your place in God's waiting room yet
He's still on your case, I'm willing to bet
Try to be active, do all that you can
And trust your next step is part of His plan

FREEDOM
BOB KIMMERLING (71)

The somersault and overswing,
the trampoline and horse.
Once knees and calves still had their spring
and strength to run their course.
While back and bones are sore and ache
to meet my day from bed,
and hips take time to floor my feet,
my mind goes there instead,
I will the ball to net.
I dance and run, I score a try,
I swim, I dive - and better yet,
I take off, and I fly.
The day will come when greater ease
allows me from this stall.
Spirit body then will please
without restraint or fall -
and whistle's end to mortal games
won't be my boundary wall.

HERE'S TO OLD AGE AND A NEW BEGINNING
ANGELA DAVEY (57)

You're getting older, perhaps with trepidation
But change that feeling to one of elation;
There's plenty of life to look forward to
With fun to be had and creative activities to do,
While some like to natter and to knit
Others run marathons or have ways to keep fit;
There's no need to worry about "dodgy knees"
When you can do whatever you please,
Bedtime can be early or be late
And there's no need to get up way before eight,
It's a myth it's all wrinkles and grey hair
When we live life to the full and without a care;
Our lessons from life we're happy to impart
And our help and advice comes from the heart,
We'll always offer a listening ear
And we find time to help others and to volunteer,
Our diaries fill up weeks in advance
So of a last minute arrangement, there's probably no
    chance;
It's not the start of the end when we grow old
Instead it's a time for adventures and when we can be
    bold
There's no holding us back and we'll face our fears
As there's a lot to pack in to our final years
They say the best years of your life are when you're at
    school
But being old is really quite cool.

HOPE IN AGEING
*POETRY GROUP AT PRICEHOLME MHA CARE
HOME**

Despite joints that ache
And skin that now flakes
We hope we'll enjoy good health
Despite knees that creak
And bladders that leak
We hope we'll enjoy good health
Though memory might dim
And hair might go thin
We hope we'll enjoy good health

If our children need aid
And our bills need to be paid
We hope we'll have adequate wealth
To pay for our care
We need to beware
That we'll need to have adequate wealth
To go out and have fun
Now our work days are done
We hope we'll have adequate wealth

BUT – We get such great care
And kindness folk share,
And we often turn back to our faith.
So more than our health
And far more than wealth
Hope in ageing comes from faith

That we'll have eternal life,
A life free from strife,
When to Heaven we go one and all.
God's promise will come true
For me and for you
When He finally gives us the call.

PATSY MAYNARD (97), MARY DYSON (83), EDITH LIVESEY (87), DIANE MCDONALD (77), EDNA OXLEY (82), MARY FEUERHELM (95), PHYLLIS DEKTEREFF (94), SHIRLEY HEPWORTH (87), HILDA HUBBARD (89), JOAN BOULD (99), CHAPLAIN RUTH DALE (76)

HOPE IN AGEING
LOIS WILTSHIRE (70)

As we grow older, what can we share,
Experience, encouragement and always a prayer,
We have survived all these years right up to now,
Happy times, sad times, we have lots to tell.
With faith, we have Hope of the life to come,
When sorrow and sickness will all be done,
In our hearts is Eternity, the Bible says so,
Placed there by our Father so long ago.
We have time on our hands to give to the youth,
Our faith brought us here, of that we have proof,
Give our time to listen, our faces to smile,
Making memories with others is always worthwhile.
The Hope of Heaven is what keeps us going,
So let us share Jesus, His love keep on sowing.

Hope in Ageing is vital to me,
Without such hope – oh where would I be!

HOPE IN AGEING ACROSTIC
CHRISTINE TRUSCOTT (73)

Health is important
Opportunities arise,
Places to go,
Enjoyment to realise.

Indulgence to savour,
Not in a hurry.

Adventures to enjoy,
Grandchildren to love,
Excitement to experience,
Interests to learn,
Nature to enjoy,
Grateful to be alive.

HOPE IN AGEING. BREAD.
HERMIONE ROFF (75)

I try not to eat the bread of
Yesterday, with its bitter herbs of
Regret and sorrow.
I go instead to buy bread of
Today, it's warm damp smell
Curling like hopeful fires inside me.
As for the bread of
Tomorrow – the
Bread of the morrow will
Always be there to find.

In my foolishness I thought, 'There will
Always be bread of tomorrow,' but
Santa Maria dictated otherwise.

The bakery was open, and
There was a baker. He
Looked at me and said,
"Today is the Feast Day of Santa Maria. I have
No bread of today but I have kept the
Bread of yesterday. I have it
Carefully wrapped. It is
Soft." I took the
The bread of yesterday, with its
Bitter herbs of regret and sorrow, and
Carefully I re-examined it. The
Bread of yesterday became my

Hope in Ageing

Bread of today – soft and malleable,
Good to break, good to chew again.

We should remember that the
Bread of yesterday may become the
Bread of today, the bread with which, as the
Waters roll over our head, we
Leave this world for the morrow.

HOPE IN AGEING RAP
JANE MENNIE (68)

I look in the mirror to check my hair,
Is that my mother that I see there?
Her lovely face, her thick white curls?
Her Sunday suit, her string of pearls.

At the age I am now I see the parents I recall.
There must be hope in ageing for us all,
If we can forgive ourselves, because we didn't see,
The important need for independence and privacy,
Balanced with a need for chat and company.
We couldn't understand that because we were young
     and busy,
With our minds on work and a growing family.
But now there is dawning a new reality,
As we move into the age of different possibilities…

Is that me napping after lunch as soon as I sit down?
And using my bus pass to take me to town?
Taking tablets, needing help with I.T?
Scrolling through the rubbish looking for something
     decent on T.V?

My hope in ageing is that my eyesight will stay,
Good enough to read the Bible each day,
That I won't get despondent and fed up with living.
I want to be grateful for each day that God is giving.

Hope in Ageing

In the family photo at the top of the stairs,
I see all of my little ones seated there.
God's gift to us of the new generations,
A bit of us in all of them, individual combinations.

At the age we are now, there's a lot we can recall.
There must be hope in ageing for us all,
If we can see ourselves in them when we were their
     ages.
Love ourselves as we turn back the pages.
Be patient with "little me" as we are with them,
Look back with love rather than condemn.
With our minds, prayers, phones on our growing
     family.
They are forming lives of new opportunity,
In a world for us all of endless possibilities…

And how we love it when we can teach them,
Play with them, read to them, chat to them.
Hear about boyfriends and homework and jobs,
Put up a hem, go for a walk with the dogs.
Send them a text, be interested in their day…

My hope in ageing is that I will always know how to
     pray,
For each of the children, each step of the way.
That I won't get cross when we don't agree,
But always be grateful for family.
At the end of the ages, standing hand in hand in
     eternity.

HOPE IN AGEING: THE WAY TO HOPE
JACQUELINE HAMBLIN (79)

'Jesus said "I am the way" ' John 14 v 6

Life is a journey, we each travel a road
From time to time we have to carry a load
Things may change, we enter a new chapter
Circumstances differ, new things come after.
No good when things go wrong to despair
Sometimes our vehicle (body) needs some repair.
We cannot stand still nor go back
Each day we move forward along the track
Old age approaches, we grow ever older
But with faith – we walk ever bolder.
The bible teaches our faith gives us hope
Trusting the lord gives us strength to cope.
Senses: memory, sight, hearing – we suffer loss
We can hope for the future – just look to the cross.
Put your trust in the saviour, no need to fear
Hope and peace can be yours each new year.
One day at a time is all he gives
Praise the lord – Jesus lives.
Trust in the lord and you will find
You will have peace of mind.

REMEMBER, JESUS SAID, "I AM THE WAY"

HOPE WITHIN
BRENDAN CONBOY (63)

You age, degrade, and rage as life fades
Is this the way to behave?
With one foot in the grave?
Feeling dismayed
Want your life replayed
Need to be brave
Grow old with dignity
Maintain your integrity
Embrace creativity
Forget about your vanity
Hold on to your sanity
Hold on to the hope within
It's never too late to begin
A new pastime
Expand your mind
Write a poem in rhyme
Seek and you shall find
Always be kind
Do not mope
Get off the slippery slope
We all have hope
No matter your stage or age
Do not be afraid
Hope will always drive out fear
Hope will wipe away your tear
Hope sustains you every year
Always keep hope near

HOPES AND DREAMS
JENNY BETTERIDGE (70)

Yesterday, when I was young
I thought I knew it all
Living life in the fast lane
I was riding for a fall.

Then when I grew older
And had children of my own
I was much too busy
To care for those living alone.

And when the children left
To build a life of their own
What a big adjustment!
They'd gone, but I mustn't moan.

I filled my life with friends and hobbies
No time left to spare
I was getting older
But determined not to care.

What happened to the hopes and dreams
That I had yesterday?
Had they all passed me by
As time slipped away?

But now that I am very old
When I'm feeling sad

Hope in Ageing

I think of all the gifts I have
Life can't be all that bad.

I have so much to make me happy
The first crocus of spring
The warmth of the sunshine
As I listen to the blackbird sing.

The sunshine makes us smile
So much to be grateful for
I dream of happy summer days
And hope for many more.

HOROLOGY
ROSE MARMION (56)

First of all the liver spots,
Like mini tea stains popping up.
I'm sure they weren't there yesterday.
O how I wish they'd go away!
Spider veins adorn my face,
A scattered web of crimson lace.
My rolling gait! Like, what the heck?
Stiffened back and stiffer neck.

Random grunts to sit and rise,
And reading blurs with failing eyes.
Balance now I seem to lack.
I'm not sure when I lost the knack.
And what has happened to my skin?!
From baby smooth to paper thin.
And moments when my words get garbled;
Lord, don't let me lose my marbles.

Ageing may sound pretty naff,
But wait, let's sift the wheat from chaff.
I look back now, and I can see
How all this change is meant to be.
Though days be long and years be short,
There's much in life that I've been taught:
Things good and bad, the highs, the falls,
That age is never promised all.

Hope in Ageing

Mistakes I've made, good choices too;
I've wisdom I can pass to you:
That whilst I age and seem to fade,
I'm not entirely in the shade.
There's still more life in this old dog yet,
Much more to do, so don't you fret.
A journey's planned that excites my heart,
Though I've no set date when I might depart.

But when I leave, as I surely will,
My heart's desire will be fulfilled.
When it's time to go and the shadows loom,
My Saviour Christ will steer me home.

I MAY BE OLDER
JACKIE CURTIS (53)

I may be older,
I may have wrinkles,
I may be slower,
But I have hope in ageing.
I may have physical limitations,
I may not do as much,
I may remember less,
But I have hope in ageing.
I am still a valued person,
I am still the beloved of God,
Created in his image,
I have hope in ageing.
I have feelings of hope and fear,
I still have all manner of feelings,
I am still on a journey with Jesus,
I have hope in ageing.
I have some wisdom and experience,
But I am still able to learn new things,
We never know everything no matter our age,
I have hope in ageing.
I still have a desire to be closer to Jesus,
Soaking in his presence,
To be more peaceful and loving,
I have hope in aging.
Wrinkled hands
And wrinkled faces
Oh but what I know!

Hope in Ageing

Now I am old I can stop, look and smell,
Enjoying their beauty, God sure made them well!
Now I don't need to order my day by the clock,
I can wait on the Lord, be still and take stock.

I don't feel old.
When I look in the mirror, I might look old.
But I don't feel old.
Though I am old I can still sing,
Raising my voice in praise to my king.
I can lift up my hands and worship my God.
Giving thanks for his presence, as I've walked this long
    road.

I'M STILL ME!

SUSAN WHITEFORD (72)

So, my body don't look like it used to,
But I'm still the same soul inside.
And although it might take me longer,
I still like to dress with pride.

My fingers are crooked, sometimes they're sore.
But they can still close in a prayer.
And they can hold the hand of a grandchild,
And show them how much I care.

Lines have appeared all over my face
I'm up 3 or 4 times every night,
But I have so much to be grateful for,
I can honestly say, it's alright!

The topic is illness when meeting with friends
But we're thankful for medicines and pills.
We have a good laugh, mainly at ourselves,
When sorting the "on-line" bills.

I can't walk as much as I used to
But then I can still drive my car.
Cyberspace, Instagram, podcasts,
Is technology's going too far!

If I can't get out, I chat on the phone
It's good to keep feeling cheery.

Hope in Ageing

And if all else fails and there's no-one in,
I can talk to Alexa or Siri.

I wear sensible shoes, no longer high heels,
I have to draw in my eye-brow.
My hair is short, not the colour it was.
But, grey hair's in fashion now

I need glasses to read, and really good light.
I'm usually in bed before 10.
But when I wake in the morning I say, "Thank you
      Lord",
And it's, here we go again!

The lady you see before you,
Is the same girl she was in her youth.
Happy, blessed and content with her lot,
And grounded in Biblical truth.

IN HOPE WE TRUST
ELIZABETH HARRISON (70+)

Be praised that, you still 'kick about'.
When possible, scream or shout,
Sing or dance, or be a basket,
You'll be long enough, within a casket?
Make sure you clean, your pearly whites,
Lest gum infection, on them alights.
'Thanks Be, to Grand-kids', you may say?
'They'll not prevent that holiday'.
In their love, they bring their joys,
Broken noses, roses, shins or toys.
That sciatic pain, is not a curse,
You got that chat, with the pretty nurse?
When dog attached, to invalid car,
People say 'Hello', ask how you are,
'I'm alright, it's the other joggers,
The Saturday crowds and daily Bloggers'.
Old Age Hope, is not just that,
It is the barber, visits, our dog, or cat.
The dipped rich-tea, new, newspaper,
The gossip on the High Road, usual caper,
Walking the golf-course, with the pals,
Singsong, keep-fit club, with the gals.
The late nights and the late arise,
The Summer sunshine, a great surprise,
The greenhouse and its tenants little,
Verdant 'sprouts', preparing to vittle.
The Easter Service, greeting old hands,

Hope in Ageing

The UK bunting and the UK brass bands,
The UK Christmas cards, carols and lights,
Visiting London and its historical sites.
Where there is Hope, there is Life they say,
Enjoy it to the fullest, to the very last day.

KEEP SMILING
CONNIE APPS (76)

If you're feeling lonely, take a tip from me.
Count all your blessings, whatever they may be.

Try to remember all that gave you joy,
When you were a child that very special toy.

A very treasured moment with family or a friend,
Hold on to that memory, never let it end.

The sight of a butterfly flitting here and there,
A very busy bumblebee who doesn't really care.

Make someone happy every single day,
The joy you give to them will soon come back your
way.

LESS CONSEQUENCE
MARIA THERESE WILLIAMS (54)

Now, finally comes more time for daydreams; tools
down, getting some guilt-free head space
Let the youngsters chase the deadlines and compete in
the consumer-race
Judgement has retreated on what we say and how we
dress
The chance to dance at any moment without the need
to look "perfect"
More time to read the children stories and ponder over
butterflies
Time to build giant sandcastles and look for faces in
the sky
Finger-painting's much more fun without pressure to
clear the mess
You feel no need for competition, what will be, will be,
we'll do our best
We've grown in appreciation of our bodies and their
worth
Preoccupied in their endurance rather than their
growth.
Age brings liberation from the targets all around
And we can sit back and so enjoy the freedom that
we've found

LIFE'S SPAN
SUE WHALLEY (66)

Youthful, blooming, able, energetic.
This was my life BC – before children!
And as a young mum it continued.
Exciting times as my growing family
Gained independence and wisdom.
Each era providing its own challenges,
Joys, heartaches and dramas.

I was unconsciously ageing in a haze of happiness
Until an event extinguished the future I'd envisaged.
Suddenly looking ahead was bleak,
As offspring now embarked on paths of their own
And I was left to grow older alone,
Without a life's partner.
Bereft, rudderless, robbed.

But life goes on – nothing is truer
And grief lessens its bony grasp.
New roads are carved out,
Taken with courage and resilience,
If a little hesitation and nervousness.
Friends become dearer and closer
And companionship is vital and valued.

There is now a whole new outlook and vision.
A new lease of vitality and verve.
With ageing comes a desire

Hope in Ageing

To live life to the full and time
Left on the clock takes on a special significance.
Creaky hips, spectacled eyes, grey hair,
All seek to create a good to be alive vibe!

There is rhythm, there is space.
There is room to share with my grandchildren.
I have a comfy lap, arms to hug, a voice to read.
Imagination enough to soar with them
As we join in make-believe games.
The sweetest sound in the world
Is 'Grandma, come and play'!

LUXURIOUS LEISURE
JANE BROCKLEHURST (68)

If the day starts without me
I can sit in bed and "chill".
It doesn't mean I'm lazy
And it doesn't mean I'm ill.

I check social media
– that phrase makes me want to smile –
think it through and pray it through
as I puzzle for a while.

Each day is ordinary,
though my days are always full
with things that really matter,
little things, but never dull.

Conversations, cups of tea,
a slice of chocolate cake,
cards handwritten just for me,
and laughing until I shake.

Never underestimate,
giving thanks at the day's end
for small kind acts and kind words,
the great value of a friend.

MATRYOSKA

EIRENE FARGHER-SMITH (76)

I hold my newborn grandchild in my arms.
Gaze into the deep lacuna of her eye
And try to fathom how it is. Could be,
That we two are not strangers, she and I.
Somewhere deep and visceral an ancient truth
Comes and comes again from long ago
That when her mother grew deep within me
My body made the ova she would someday be.
And so, by God's incredible design,
The magical potential of that life to be
Was, in its turn, once seeded in the womb
Of she who had conceived and nurtured me.
Therefore, no stranger to my grand-daughter I'll be.
Matryoska like each generation stands alone
Yet holds within herself the female line
Just as my grandmother held me one time.
And in this perfect synchronicity of life
Despite the fact that I am worn and old
I know that by this life affirming truth
The essence of my story will be told.

['Matryoshka' means 'mother' in Russian and is the
name for Russian nesting dolls which, originally, were
a homage to fertility and family.]

MY HOPE

NEIL COOPER (76)

The hope I have is not my own
It comes from Him upon His throne,
This hope was not just there for me,
It came from Him upon that tree.
It is the hope that's there for all,
We needed it from Adam's fall,
We were lost until He stepped in
And took on Himself our weight of sin.
My Hope is not just what He said,
But that He is risen from the dead,
And that He promised we could be
With Him in eternity,
If we accepted what He'd done
And on that cross our victory won,
Our saviour Jesus, Lord of all
Who said 'just on Me call
And I will cross eternity,
To bring You home to be with Me.

MY NEW ME
ANGIE POLLARD (68)

I really thought I'd had it: my future looked so grim.
I'd hit the dreaded five-oh: I was no longer thin.
I hadn't LOST my figure, it just upped and left one
     day.
But I've become so much more cuddly, and that's a lot
     to say.

I'm finding much more patience; I'm delighted to be
     calmer;
When things go somewhat pear-shaped I respond with
     nervous laughter.
The little things that niggled have vanished overnight.
I'm so happy to be older, I'm glad I've given up the
     fight.

So now that I am 'more mature', when I don't get my
     way,
I smile and think it over – there's still another day.
Another day to get involved in bigger things than
     these.
To join the fight 'gainst climate change or save
     dolphins in the seas.

So life is just commencing, my future's just begun.
I've resolved to make a difference. Now, look out,
     everyone!

NEVER STOP LEARNING
ALEXANDRA WILDE (77)

Looking back over more than fifty years,
As a lass of twenty-two
The whole world was my oyster,
With everything fresh and new.
Back then, I thought I knew the lot
And could always hold my own
In any argument or debate:
My English skills I'd hone.

Now, it's clear, I've learned so much
But, as the seasons turn,
I realise that the more I know
The more I've still to learn!
For life's a long, hard road to ride –
You're tempered by the fire
Rough edges smoothed, until at last
You reach your heart's desire.

OLD AGE ISN'T SO BAD
PATRICIA HAMMERSLEY (72)

Old age isn't so bad you know
Because like me you can let things go
I don't let fashion dictate to me
I wear the things that I please

I don't have to worry about being home late
Especially if I'm out on a date
My food is ordered all online
And Google is great for passing the time
I have plenty of friends that come and go
That my time never goes slow

I fill each day with things that please
My knitting and crotchet and making tea
It's nice to meet friends and have a chat
There's plenty to say about this and that

Time is precious so don't let it slip by
So at the end you won't want to cry
Live every moment as though it's your last
And if you can, fill it with laughs

OLDER? HOW DARE YOU!

ELIZABETH A ALI (68)

How dare my feet not want to go
To where my mind remembers so,
To scramble up a heather moor,
Picking bilb'rries - not anymore!

How dare you pose me such a question!
Nothing's faulty with my vision.
What's that Officer, did you say?
Oops, I've parked in a loading bay!

How dare my children tell me I
Have the TV volume up sky high.
Go see the Audiologist?
Okay, I'll add it to my list.

How dare my mind deceive me so,
Pretending details I don't know,
Besides, I have a scroll somewhere
That proves I know it all, so there!

How dare you say I'm negative,
Or say I'm argumentative,
At least I still know how to be
Cantankerous, difficult me!

. . . .

Hope in Ageing

Maybe I've just overstated
That my life has dissipated
Into something less than worthwhile,
Let us view a different profile.

Leading through the heather, Grandma
Teaches where the bilberries are,
Purple-mouthed grandchildren learn
Names of the birds down by the burn.

How about our expedition
To a far-flung destination,
Doubts dispelled within a jiffy
In a rain-forest so pretty.

Learning Spanish, Arabic, French,
Investing in a new workbench,
Visiting friends, both old and new,
So many stunning things to do.

Finding new adventures, surely,
Is the future for the weary,
Even if our bodies fail us,
Don't let doubt of self derail us.

ONCE A CREATIVE
CHRISTINE RATCLIFF (86)

Our parish group is planning an Event –
"Inspiring Creativity" the main intent.
"Sign here if you can offer something arty.
We need your help for our amazing party."
You sign, they smile, ask, condescendingly:
"Perhaps you'd like to help to pour the tea?"

Reply: "No fear!" (They look like they'd been shot.)
"Aren't you thinking I might drop the pot?
But lead me to the maypole – I can dance.
I'd be on Strictly, given half a chance.
And on that shelf - if you would care to look,
you'll see my poems published in a book.
Pass me my guitar, I'll sing a song…"

They think we've had our day. But they are wrong!

RECIPE FOR A HAPPIER OLD AGE
ANGIE POLLARD (68)

Ingredients

As much hope as you can gather.
Lashings of kindness – several pounds at least.
Liberal dollops of laughter.
A measure (you can have too much of a good thing) of uncontrollable giggles.
365 sunrises.

Method

Melt and stir the hope vigorously with your 'Things WILL Get Better' spoon. It may seem hard and unyielding at first, but persevere: the Mixing Bowl of Life can take it.
Set aside for a while, adding lashings of kindness as frequently as possible. If you run out, make a trip to the shops for more. You can never have enough.
Take time to stir in liberal dollops of laughter at intervals.
Find some friends*. Sit on a bench with the uncontrollable giggles.
Add in a smile at each sunrise, every single day. Even when you can't see the sun (you often won't).
Pour into your life and bake at a gentle heat for 24 hours, 7 days a week, 52 weeks a year.
Yes, it does take time.
Enjoy**.

(**Horrible word, but it's modern. We need to go with the flow.)
Note: all measurements are in 'old money'. I'm surely not the only BM (Before Metric) human alive in the UK.

*Can't find any friends? Make new ones. They are available at many outlets, including supermarkets, small shops, libraries, buses, parks. Own/borrow a dog if necessary.

SELF-SUFFICIENCY
ALI MITCHELL (73)

I'm what you might call self-sufficient
And at caring for me most proficient
With a cat on my knee
And a nice cup of tea
Seems there's nothing of which I'm deficient
To romancing I'm now quite resistant
With no suitors at present persistent
I work best on my own
Like a queen on her throne
With romantic intentions far distant
To my critics I'm rarely compliant
My track-record is being defiant
I've spent too many years
Wasted too many tears
Feeling harassed and too acquiescent
I'm not quite the lady omniscient
But at gathering gossip consistent
It's not just that I'm curious
But it does seem more spurious
To impart news that proves inefficient
My children have moved on insistent
That I'll make it because I'm belligerent
But how little they know
Just how slow time can go
When close mingling is so intermittent
Too many old friendships have gone
As time passes and people move on

Embracing Age

So I'm counting my blessings
And learning new lessons
Until ageing is finally done
For a catch up please make an appointment
In a bid to avoid disappointment
When you visit you'll see
That I'm still the old me
Ageing nicely with gracious contentment

SOUL REFLECTIONS
JEREMY WINTER (64)

I sit on a bench in the sunny spot
Watching the shadows and pools of light
A day of conversations and friendship
But also of solitude and empty space

Time to reflect, as the sun, still warm
Goes down in its usual, ever-changing place
Warming my body and comforting my soul
Giving me confidence and courage to face the night

And after night, another day
With, as yet, unknown experiences
Predictable, but often full of surprises
A day to be thankful, because I'm alive

Healing comes in the morning
When everything is new and starts again
The hurts and pain of yesterday
Forgotten or lessened in intensity
As the sunrise says "take my hand"

THANK YOU DEAREST EMILY
HELEN MASON (78)

Thank you dearest Emily
For sending cards so joyfully
You have become my family
Now daughter moved across the sea

I worked with children to inspire
I never wanted to retire
You rescued me in my old age
Life is a book - I'd turned a page

I needed help so desperately
I was as lonely as can be
Retirement had been forced on me
With its utmost cruelty.

You have worked so tirelessly
Devoted your whole life to me
You gave us hope, you gave us peace
Our loneliness began to cease.

Now we begin each day anew
We plan what we are going to do
Meet our befriender, have a chat
We'll feel much better after that.

My befriender phones me every week
It is a joy to hear her speak

Hope in Ageing

She has a full time job to do
But makes time to include me too

Our lives have changed dramatically
I've got a friend who welcomes me
The time now passes pleasantly
As we await our destiny

Thank you dearest Emily
For all that you have done for me
You've given us tranquillity
with your love and sympathy

You have become so close to me
My very dearest Emily
Transformed your life so you can see
How to help the elderly

I now give thanks for Emily
Who rescued many just like me
Now joined together peacefully
Like one big loving family

[Emily Kenward founded Time to Talk Befriending to
link elderly lonely people with a befriender]

THE JOURNEY
OLIVE GRIFFIN (98)

Much is said about growing old
Some of it is true
But when it comes to you my friend
You'll have a different view

For life has many ups and downs
And does not go to plan
The dreams you had when very young
Have all gone down the pan

But life goes on and on it seems,
Old age is not for me
The days fly by – I'm busy, so
I do not see time flee

So much to ask,
The young can Google it, but
Technology has passed me by:
I face a daunting task

My days are nearly over.
But I wake up every morn'
Saying thanks for life
… and the sight of another dawn.

THE JOYS OF GETTING OLD
JEAN CARTER (81)

You may have heard the saying "it's the joys of getting
     old",
It's said when you're not well or even have a cold.
But there are other joys that need to be told.
Memories of family and friends, so many happy days.
Count all of your blessings and walk in God's ways.
It's no use staying at home to mope,
Get out, trust in the Lord and always have hope.
Just look at the world around you,
Find pleasure in all you see and do,
You'll find life still has a lot to give,
So embrace "the joys of getting old" and live.

THE POINT OF AGE
PAUL BLACKETT (59)

What's the point of age?
Aches and pains bring,
Tablets and potions,
Slow mornings and sleepless nights.

What's the point of age?
Wrinkles and lines,
New joints and teeth,
Diaries filling with appointments.

I know the point of age,
Experiences lived,
Laughs at memories,
Photographs shared over coffee.

I know the point of age,
When to plant seeds,
How to check tyres,
Stories sat on older knees.

I know the point of age,
How to make knots,
Where to find berries,
Small hands held and trusting.

I know the point of age,
Buckets and spades,

Hope in Ageing

While parents away,
Wisdom shared to younger ears.

The years don't count,
But memories do,
Tell stories, share laughs,
The Hope is in you.

THE TOUCH OF A HAND
JULIE JORDAN (64)

There's a dear old lady who rests in her chair,
She's fast asleep it seems.
They quietly stop to linger there,
Then leave her to her dreams.

But she's not really deeply asleep.
She's silently deep in prayer.
She's asking God to watch over and keep
All those who give her daily care.

She knows they've no time to stay awhile,
Nor stop by for a chat,
But she always loves to watch with a smile
As they talk about this and that.

She calls them angels in disguise,
As they gently stroke her hair.
But they don't see the faraway look in her eyes
She knows God puts angels everywhere.

'Would you like a lovely cup of tea?'
One of those sweet angels said.
She laughed and gently said, 'you see
It's a long time since I had my tea in bed'.

'I once was young like you' she said,
'But the circle of life turned too fast.

Hope in Ageing

Although there is still a child in my head
That wants to cling onto the past'.

'When you're young you're dressed and told
The places you have to go.
It's just the same when you get to be old
Though now you're all stooped and slow'.

'One day you too will be old like me
And then you will understand,
That all you really hope for, you see
Is the gentle touch of a hand'.

THERE IS ALWAYS NEW HOPE
HOLLY TRUNDLE (56)

Old feet walk paths to new horizons,
Making fresh friendships along the way.
Past experience adds perspective,
Expanding knowledge through U3A,
Social groups, belly dancing or Men's Sheds,
University, workshops, or boisterous grandchildren.
Concession advantage helps us with bus tickets,
Mature Student railcards: teen to 25 again.
Stretch your grey pound for concerts and daytrips,
Opening doors to new styles and old favourites –
Tate Modern Gallery, Gilbert and Sullivan, Ed Sheeran,
Take That, Janette Mason, and films at the flicks,
Hikes along clifftops, pints on peak pinnacles,
Or leisurely strolls through manicured gardens.
Age beyond fifty lets you take liberties,
Stating your terms and having fun without pardon.
We know what we like, and what makes us grumpy,
We know how to help, but being helped is quite hard.
We have learned that the future writes its own script,
So, we might as well trust, and let Fate turn the cards.
If life is a race, we can choose how we pace it –
A dash, a slow saunter, or bike ride to the rope.
However, you view the next day, week or decade,
Life's for living, my friend, there is always new hope.

TREES

ANN SANGWIN (76)

My mother, at 88 years old,
watched the news of the tsunami
with amazement.
Everything was flattened
or swept away,
she said, except the trees.
Why did the trees remain standing?

They are like you,
I thought:
their roots are deep,
for years they have withstood
the buffeting of the elements,
the battering of the storms.
They have provided
shelter and support,
bending but not broken,
bearing the scars of hardship
and still standing.
Like you.

UNOPENED GIFT

IAN CURTRESS (96)

Half century glass so full of joy
     looking in mirrors friendly gaze
wrinkles the result of so much laughter
Smiling at the very thought
 a challenge to match
 indeed, surpass
Ready for my second phase

  But no…. really must first look back
Those memories and so much love
Perhaps there is an up above
Sadness yes we all will know
    The price we pay for Hearts capacity
to envelope such emotions…. such tenacity

All will at some point zenith reach
  And on that path life will us teach
The values of honesty to self and others
     Impenetrable shield of gossamer mist
  No words apply, one is kissed

Ribbon freed, The Gift all wishes now exceed
With such years in mirror seen
  By now you will glean, the second half
Cornucopia. Exciting possibilities
Serendipity to surprise and with a smile
Hidden talents surface, new friends beguile

Hope in Ageing

Return to mirrors warm reflection
Those laughing eyes, that smile perfection
    Fun and lovely thoughts escape
Have for so long below the surface reigned
    No longer will they be contained
A spring in step
        Infectious laugh
           Ready for the second half.

USE IT OR LOSE IT, YOU CHOOSE IT
GLENYS ADAMS (72)

Plantar fasciitis and arthritic hip,
Creaky knees and dodgy ankles all give me jip.
Rising from the sofa with sighs and grunts and groans,
Flexing aching muscles and rearranging bones,
I stand.
Feet firmly planted shoulder width apart.

And then the music starts
　　Pulsing through my pulse, p'pulse, p'pulse,
　　Pumping, rising, fizzing, filling
　　Sole to soul.
　　I step out of my stiffened frame and

　　I dip and I skip and I swirl and I twirl and
　　I jive two three four, and tap six seven eight,
　　I stamp and I stomp and I slide and I glide.
　　I tango and I foxtrot and I rumba and I salsa and
　　I waltz two three, rise two three, fall two three,
　　Fade two three,
Breathe two three
four five six
seven eight, and
　　Rest…

WHEN I AM OLD AND SPENT

ELISABETH ROSEMARY COGHLAN (77)

When I am Old and Spent
Don't stuff my head
With radio talk; so much is said
That won't be heard –
Shallow chat and tuneless music
No, don't do that!

Instead, leave me quiet to reflect
On life and friends and on the church.
Leave me silent to think and pray…
Or watch the sunlight play a dance
Dipping in and out of leaves
While they shiver in the breeze.

Don't sit me in front of the T.V. set
Where I am forced to listen to an act
Which neither cheers nor edifies.
No, the picture I prefer to see
Is the English sky with its variety
Of blue and grey and orange and white:
The cumulus clouds and the changing light
The soft wetting rain and heavy showers
That sparkle on our garden flowers.
This is the picture I would see
Not video or colour T.V.
(P.S. To Radio 3, I might agree!)

Embracing Age

The noisy starlings prepare to flight
And chattering birds settle for night
Pre-school children's innocent cry
These are the sounds that delight my senses.

Please let a friend pay a visit
To sit with me, or sometimes speak
Of their activities, or walk with me
And just be a friend.

I watch mankind walking by
(it's life in motion)
Each one is precious in God's eye
Have they a notion
Of how much he loves them?
When I am old, I'd like to see
Such people walk in front of me.

WHEN I WAS BORN

HENK VAN OORT

When I was born
my backpack was almost too full,
so laden with my future years.

When I was born
my backpack was almost too full,
so laden with my hidden tears.

When firmly on my way I covered quite a mile
and lingered for a while
in towns and places
among many loving faces.

At this old age, so well advanced,
I take quite another stance.

Now my point of view is mountain high.
The target, so I feel, is looming nigh.

The burden on my back feels feather light;
the summit clearly comes in sight.

Every task became
a spark of wisdom
on my journey to where I came from.

Every meeting turned into

a Flame of Love
and
slowly, slowly, I awaken to this
Realm of Light
above.

WHEN WE LEAST EXPECT IT
JOHN BUXTON (58)

Hope as we age comes when we least expect it
first light through undrawn curtains
enthused by the rising of the sun
it is present in every heart beat giving life and energy
it arrives in a misty coloured rainbow after a
      thunderous storm
it greets us in a stranger's warm smile as we stroll
a loved one's happy voice overseas
just close enough to bring comfort and joy
hope as we age comes in the aroma of the Hyacinth
      flower
vibrant, intoxicating, a delight to behold
it comes in the chuckle from a new born baby
the intrigue of a kitten or puppy
the taste of a sweet tangerine.

Hope as we age arrives in the simplicity and beauty of
      birdsong
the warm reassuring glow of candlelight
fresh laundered linen, the smell of a new book
it comes in meaningful appreciation of others, of our
      friends
of shared laughter and of camaraderie
in wellbeing wishes for those most vulnerable
where compassion and loving kindness
eagerly await to restore our faith in humanity

hope as we age comes when we least expect it
in the joy of shared new beginnings
in seasonal awakenings of nature's perfection
in the celebration for all we are and have been
hope arrives in abundance as we seize the miracle of a
    new day.

YOUR WAY
WILLIAM BARNETT (72)

And now, my end on earth is near,
I state my case and make it clear;
My heart is full as I want to say
'My Lord, my God, I did it Your way.

And here for me no final curtain,
My faith in You is ever certain;
My tears are more for Your sacrifice,
For You paid for me my hopeless price.

I hid my fears and lived in doubt
The darkness fell - what the way out?
You carried me and showed the way,
My Lord, my God, I did it Your way.

Regrets and wrongs? More than a few!
But then I passed them all to You;
I trusted far in Your forgiving,
And took Your path in blessed living.

Within Your arms I felt Your ease,
The gift of Grace and perfect peace.
In Scripture and continued prayer
I found my voice, Your truth to share.

From shallow tunes I turn aside,
My joyful song with You abides;

Embracing Age

When eyes at last will softly close,
My love, my praise will always grow.

Our time on earth is surely brief,
But Jesu's Love shall never cease;
Let's live so all will want to say
'My Lord, my God, I did it Your way.'

ACKNOWLEDGEMENTS

"Let's run a poetry competition on the theme of 'Hope in Ageing' and publish all the shortlisted poems in an anthology!" she said, with absolutely no experience of poetry competitions or publishing.

Turning a crazy idea into reality takes a team, and at Embracing Age we are hugely grateful to everyone who has played their part, and joined us on our steep learning curve. Firstly, huge thanks to Pam Harrison, who volunteered her assistance from the outset and helped to shape and drive the whole project. Then Pam Rhodes, whose encouragement, enthusiasm and support spurred us on. Liz Windaybank, who pointed Pam Harrison in our direction, and helped us with shortlisting and proofreading. Roz de Lord, our admin volunteer at Embracing Age, who has been so willing to do whatever was thrown at her to keep things on schedule. Our wonderful judges, Pam Rhodes, Dave Bilbrough and Amanda Root – not an easy task to choose the winning poems from so many wonderful entries. Thank you for taking the time to read the poems, and deliberate over them, and for all your encouragement along the way. Holly Trundle, who graciously pointed out all our grammatical errors when the winning poems were published on our website, and then offered to proofread the book manuscript.

And finally, we are so grateful for all the poets who took the brave step of entering the competition. We have loved reading all your poems. You have made us smile, you have brought tears to our eyes and you have warmed our hearts. Thank you.

ABOUT EMBRACING AGE

We're a Christian charity that's all about older people. We want to encourage a positive view of getting older, hence our theme of "Hope in Ageing". We want our communities and our churches to be great places to grow old.

We're working towards a world where older people are valued, respected and full of hope. We recognise that sometimes in our advancing years frailty can develop, causing us to be more dependent than perhaps we would like. But physical and cognitive decline don't diminish our worth, and we are determined to embrace those journeying through frailty with love, kindness and esteem.

We have three main strands to our work: befriending care home residents, supporting informal carers and equipping churches in their work with older people. If you want to find out more, please visit our website or contact us:

embracingage.org.uk
info@embracingage.org.uk

EMBRACING AGE
Later life in all its fullness

Printed in Great Britain
by Amazon

28198739R00066